HANDS OF THE RAIN FOREST

The Emberá People of Panama

RACHEL CRANDELL

Christy Ottaviano Books

Henry Holt and Company

NEW YORK

The Emberá of the Rain Forest

Nicaragua

Costa Rica

Panama Canal

Panama

Panama City

Darién

Sambú River

Colombia

Canada

United States of America

Atlantic Ocean

Mexico

Pacific Ocean

Caribbean Sea

Central America

South America

E
972.87
CHA
#2186

N
W   E
S

Emberá hands are seldom still. The indigenous people of Panama, the Emberá, use their hands to transform the gifts of the tropical rain forest into provisions for their families. This requires hard work and love. The Central American rain forest supplies all the basic materials, but it is the hands and hearts of the Emberá that change these plants into food, shelter, transportation, and celebration.

For centuries the Emberá lived in small family groups scattered throughout the Darién jungle where their impact on the forest was minimal. In the 1970s, the Panamanian government settled the Emberá in villages along the Sambú River. Settlement brought changes. Because so many people live closer together now, the forest and its resources are dwindling. Their gardens are farther from home. Today many families buy cooking oil and kerosene from the store in the town downriver. Their children go to school. Even so, the Emberá continue to do almost everything by hand.

When I first visited the Emberá, Ricardo, their *cacique*, chief of all chiefs, asked me to record their stories because they have no written history. He wanted the words of the old storytellers written down, so I have returned numerous times to do this work.

I vividly remember my first night in the stilt house of Eraclio, the shaman. After a supper of fried plantains and fresh river shrimp, his wife, Anatolia, told stories to her grandchildren in the dim light. The cooking fire flickered, throwing shadows across the underside of the palm leaf roof. As Anatolia's expressive hands waved dramatically, Emberá words, punctuated with sound effects, spilled out of her mouth. I sat entranced. While she told story after story, the youngest children fell asleep in the laps of their mothers. The men listened intently to the age-old stories shared once more.

Poling up the Sambú River with Manikidu in a dugout canoe to the villages deep in the Darién jungle, I have discovered a wise and caring people whose hearts are open and whose hands are skilled. The Emberá have treated me like family. I have become godmother to Mariano, and Manikidu named his new baby daughter Liana, the same name as my granddaughter. We share more than stories.

very day in an Emberá village there is work to do. Each morning you can hear the rhythmic pounding of rice. Grandmother Lenia's experienced hands lift the heavy *pestle* and drop it into the wooden *mortar* to separate the rice grains from the hulls. Children share in the work.

Cocobolo is a special wood that carvers use to create sculptures of the animals in their forest. Ramirez is carving a monkey in a forest tree. When he is finished, the wood will be as smooth as satin and glow like honey.

Ufralio has just completed his masterpiece—two crocodiles locked in battle.

Elida grates *jagua* fruit to make the juice for body painting. Mother uses the juice to decorate her daughter. The body paint turns dark in a few hours and lasts for weeks. The juice is also used as a mosquito repellent.

Rundlett Middle School
Concord, New Hampshire

Atiliano uses his *machete* to harvest *plantains*. He must clear some of the trees of the rain forest to make his plantation. He grows more than his family needs, so he can trade his crops downriver for kerosene, cooking oil, and diving masks.

Emberá families eat plantains at every meal. Mother prepares them in many different ways. For breakfast she is making *patacones* and fries them in cooking oil.

Basket making is an art. The palm leaves must be collected before they are fully open. Then they are dried and colored with natural plant dyes from the roots, bark, seeds, or pods of plants. Purple comes from the pod of the *eraka* palm.

Jaqueline plans the design of her basket before she begins weaving. She collects leaves from two different kinds of trees— *naguala* and *chunga* palm. Then she makes dyes to color the leaves. It took her a year to weave this basket.

Workbaskets are made from different palms and are not dyed. Women's capable hands have made hundreds of baskets over the years. The *pikiwa* are strong and are used to carry heavy loads of plantains, crabs, or root crops. Pani uses a *tumpline* on her basket to make it easier to carry.

At school, the teacher encourages the children to draw pictures of their homes and families, their forest and its animals.

After a morning of studies in the village school, big brothers and sisters have time to play with their little brothers and sisters.

Emberá children enjoy their pets. The pets are animals from the rain forest, like *peccary*, turtles, parrots, *paca*, deer, squirrels, and monkeys.

The children love to listen to Elio tell stories from *tiempo antiguo*. His grandfather told him these stories when he was a little boy, and his grandfather before him.

Melanio is a master *piragua* carver. It takes patience to use the *hianveh* correctly. He teaches the younger boys the work of the men. They cooperate to make a dugout canoe. It is their only transportation, and the river is their only highway.

Emberá children grow up in the forest along the river's edge.
They are excellent swimmers and must learn from their
fathers to balance standing up in a canoe while poling upriver.

Chombo is lightning fast! His spear and
diving mask help him catch the fish his
family depends on for their evening meal.
His sister cleans the fish for dinner.

The boys use the canoe poles to dig for
crabs in the riverbank. Crabs are a tasty
treat to add to the cooking pot.

The men and boys collect and fold mountains of
cortadero leaves to thatch the roof of a house.
These sturdy palm leaves shed the rain so the house
stays completely dry even in the rainy season from
May to December.

The Emberá people make music with instruments created from the rain forest. While the drummer keeps the rhythm, the flute player's nimble fingers know just which holes to cover to carry the tune.

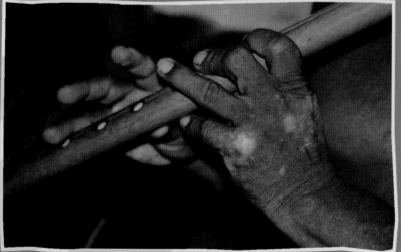

Girls love to dance. They hold on to one another's *parumas* and take turns imitating the animals of the forest. All the while, their feet stamp in time with the beat of the drum.

At the end of a long, hot day, it's time to cool off in the river. The children scrub clean in the soothing waters of the Sambú River.

The rhythm of the day's work in an Emberá village
slows at nightfall. Big brother's hands gently sway his
little brother's hammock and send him off to sleep.

GLOSSARY

CHUNGA (CHOONG a): A tall palm whose leaves are used for basket making and whose trunk is used for house posts.

COCOBOLO (ko ko BO lo): A tropical rain forest tree whose beautiful reddish color makes it desirable for carvings.

CORTADERO (kor ta DER oh): A palm whose leaves are used for roofing and can last several years.

ERAKA (EE rah kah): A tropical palm whose seed hulls make a bright purple dye when crushed and whose abundant seeds are processed to make cooking oil.

HIANVEH (hi ahn VEH): A carving tool, much like a curved adze or a chisel with a handle, used to shape the inside of a dugout canoe.

JAGUA (HAH wah): A tropical forest fruit whose clear juice turns blue-black within hours, making it perfect for body painting. It is also an insect repellent.

MACHETE (mah SHET ee): A large-bladed knife used as a tool in the tropics for planting, harvesting, carving, food preparation, hunting, house-building, and clearing forest and trails.

MORTAR (MOHR ter): A deep wooden bowl carved from a large tree. It is used for pounding rice or coffee to separate the grain or bean from its outer covering.

NAGUALA (nah WAH lah): A multipurpose tree, its leaves are used for basket making and roof thatch, and its tender young stems are edible.

PACA (PAH kah): A large nocturnal rodent relished for its delicious meat.

PARUMA (pah ROO mah): The brightly colored cloth wrap Emberá girls and women wear as a skirt. Today the cloth is made in Japan and traded for in Sambú.

PATACONES (pah tah CONE es): Plantains or wild bananas that are sliced, partially fried, smashed, and refried; a staple in the Emberá diet.

PECCARY (PECK kah ree): A wild forest pig with tusks that travels in herds in the deep forests of the Darién.

PESTLE (PEH sull): A wooden ram used for pounding grains and seeds in a mortar.

PIKIWA (pee kee WAH): A workbasket made from vine.

PIRAGUA (pee RAH wah): A dugout canoe carved from a tree, it is the usual means of river transport in remote jungle areas where there are no roads.

PLANTAIN (plan TANE): A variety of banana that is starchy and grown as a staple food crop in the tropics.

SAMBÚ (sahm BOO): The name of the river in eastern Panama that flows into the Pacific Ocean near the Colombian border. It is also the name of the main town along the Sambú River.

TIEMPO ANTIGUO (tee EM poh ahn TEE woh): The ancient times, or the period long before the Spanish came to the New World.

TUMPLINE (TUMP line): A strap attached across the forehead that is connected to a basket, making a heavy load easier to carry.

TO MANIKIDU,
whose capable hands and loving
heart have led me to friendship
with the Emberá

Henry Holt and Company, LLC
Publishers since 1866
175 Fifth Avenue
New York, New York 10010
www.HenryHoltKids.com

Library of Congress Cataloging-in-Publication Data
Crandell, Rachel.
Hands of the rain forest : the Emberá people of Panama / Rachel Crandell. —1st ed.
p.   cm. — (Christy Ottaviano books)
ISBN-13: 978-0-8050-7990-6 / ISBN-10: 0-8050-7990-4
1. Emberá Indians—Material culture. 2. Emberá Indians—Social life and customs. I. Title.
F2270.2.E43C73 2009 972.87'004989—dc22   2008038215

First Edition—2009
Designed by Meredith Pratt / Map by Jennifer Thermes
Printed in March 2009 in China by South China Printing Company Limited,
Dongguan City, Guangdong Province, on acid-free paper. ∞

1 3 5 7 9 10 8 6 4 2

Rundlett Middle School
Concord, New Hampshire